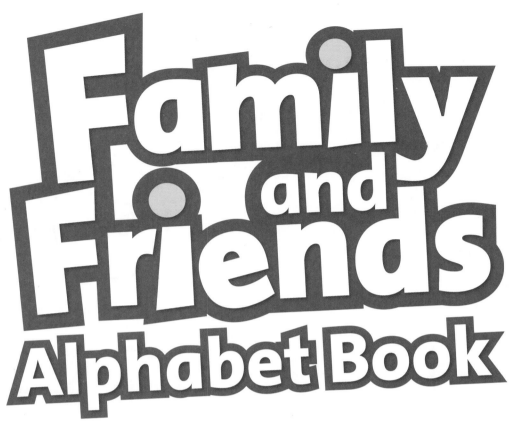

Family and Friends
Alphabet Book

T0346918

OXFORD
UNIVERSITY PRESS

Look at the alphabet.

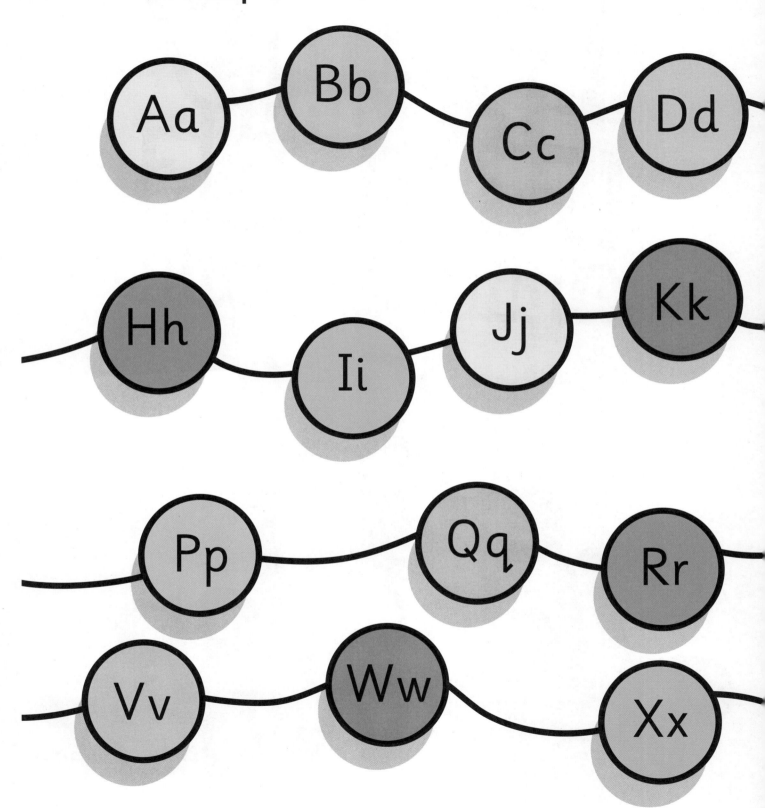

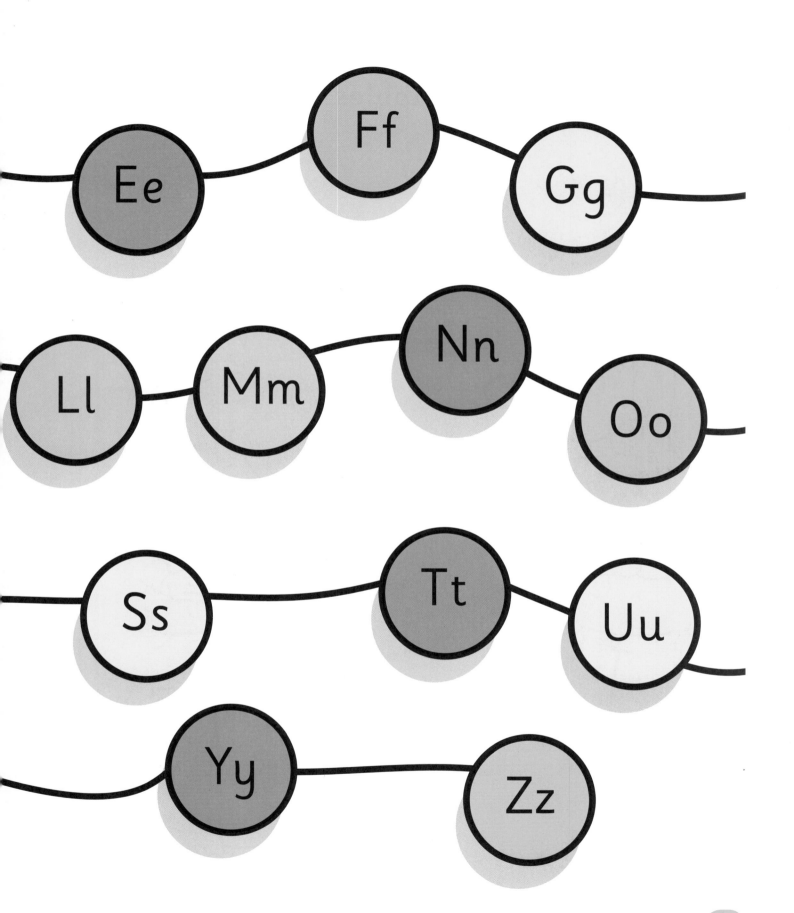

Join the letters Aa–Zz.

Who's blowing the bubbles?

Point and say the letter names you know.

Aa Bb Cc Dd Ee Ff Gg

Hh Ii Jj Kk Ll Mm Nn

Oo Pp Qq Rr Ss Tt Uu

Vv Ww Xx Yy Zz

Say the letter names. What is your name?

Find and circle the beginning letter in your name.

Ss Bb Ll Dd Pp

Ff Yy Hh Tt Rr Kk Cc Mm

Ww Oo Ee Qq Jj Aa Ii Uu

Vv Nn Xx Gg Zz

C says c in cat.

Trace

c c c c c c c

Copy

c

Copy

cat cat cat

a says a in apple.

Trace

a a a a a a a

Copy

a

Copy

apple apple pple

The cat's got an apple.

Circle your best c and c

O says o in orange.

Trace

O O O O O O O

Copy

o · · · · · ·

Copy

orange orange range

e says e in egg.

Trace

e e e e e e e

Copy

e · · · · · ·

Copy

egg egg gg

Here's an orange and an egg.

Put a ★ next to your best o and e.

Choose and tick.

 cat ☐ apple ☐ orange ☐ egg ✓

 apple ☐ orange ☐ egg ☐ cat ☐

 orange ☐ egg ☐ cat ☐ apple ☐

 egg ☐ cat ☐ apple ☐ orange ☐

Match and write.

c

a

o

e

___pple

___gg

___range

___c_at

How many ☐a s can you find?

Circle the words beginning with the letter c .

Find and circle the same letter.

c	⊙c	a	o	e	coat
a	c	a	o	e	arm
o	c	a	o	e	one
e	c	a	o	e	eye

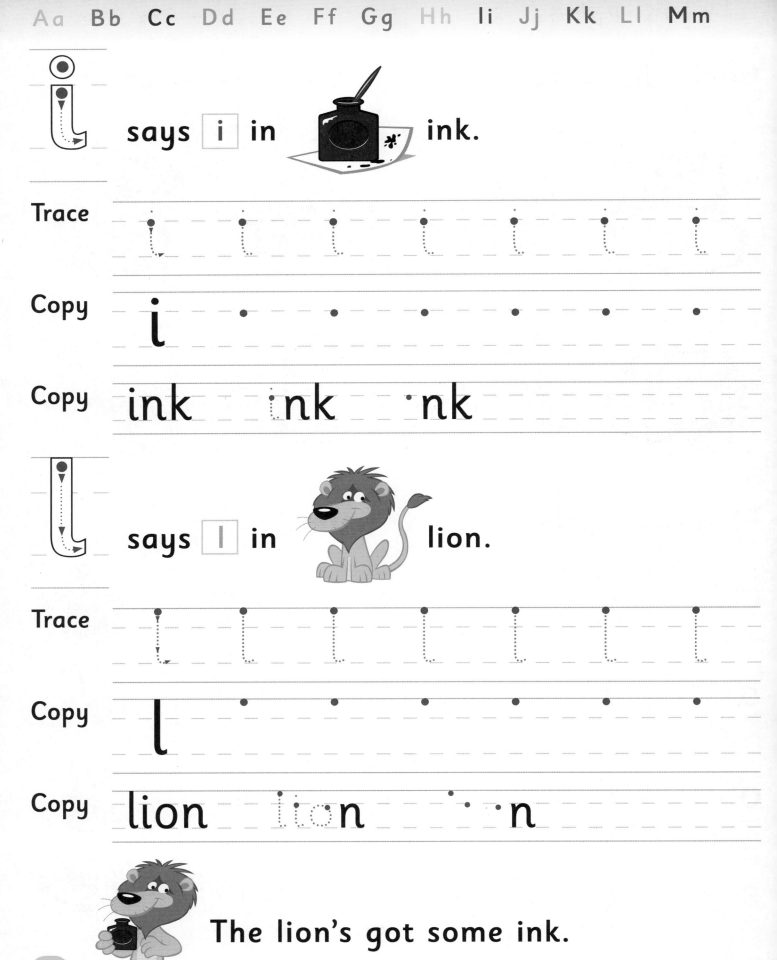

i says i in ink.

Trace

Copy   i

Copy   ink   ink   nk

l says l in lion.

Trace

Copy   l

Copy   lion   lion   n

The lion's got some ink.

Circle your best i and l

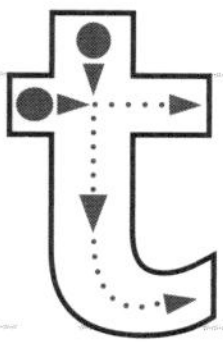

t says t in  teddy.

Trace t t t t t t t

Copy t

Copy teddy teddy ddy

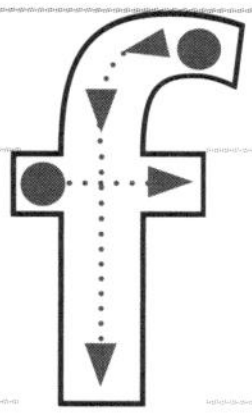

f says f in  fig.

Trace f f f f f f f

Copy f

Copy fig fig ig

The teddy's got a fig.

Circle your best t and f.

Circle and colour the correct letter.

i l t f

i l t f

i l t f

i l t f

Match and write.

i   ___ingers

l   ___en

t   ___egs

f   _i_ce cream

What other words do you know beginning with t

Match and write [t] or [f] .

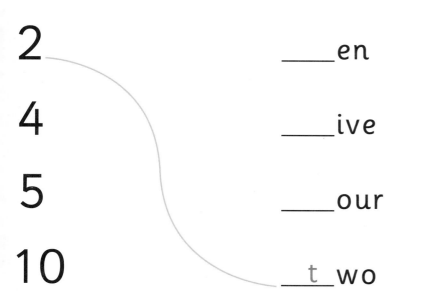

2   ____en

4   ____ive

5   ____our

10   __t_wo

Find and circle.

i	six	pink	bike	fingers
e	hello	yellow	rubber	leg
l	blue	pencil	apple	puzzle
o	window	dog	doll	nose
t	eight	cat	teacher	hat
a	bag	orange	ball	hand

What other words do you know beginning with [f]?

r says r in rabbit.

Trace r r r r r r r

Copy r · · · · · ·

Copy rabbit rabbit abbit

n says n in nurse.

Trace n n n n n n n

Copy n · · · · · ·

Copy nurse nurse urse

 **The nurse has got a rabbit.**

Circle the n s and r s in the sentenc

m says m in mum.

Trace m m m m m m m

Copy m • • • • • •

Copy mum mum um

h says h in hat.

Trace h h h h h h h

Copy h • • • • •

Copy hat hat at

This is his mum's hat.

Circle your best m and h.

15

b says b in bird.

Trace b b b b b b b

Copy b

Copy bird bird ird

p says p in pen.

Trace p p p p p p p

Copy p

Copy pen pen en

The pen is on the book.

Put a ★ next to your best b and P

Circle and colour the correct letter.

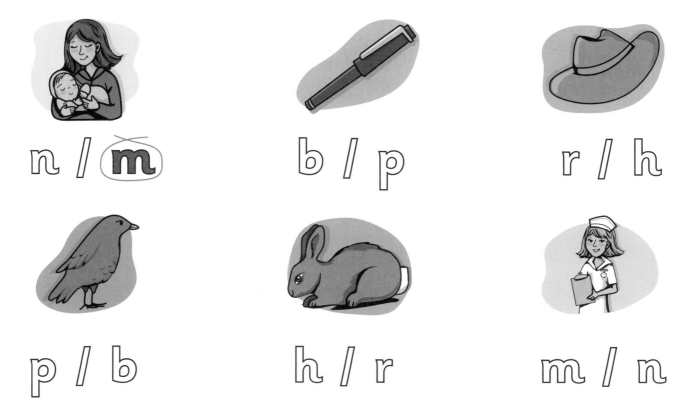

n / (m)   b / p   r / h

p / b   h / r   m / n

Choose and tick.

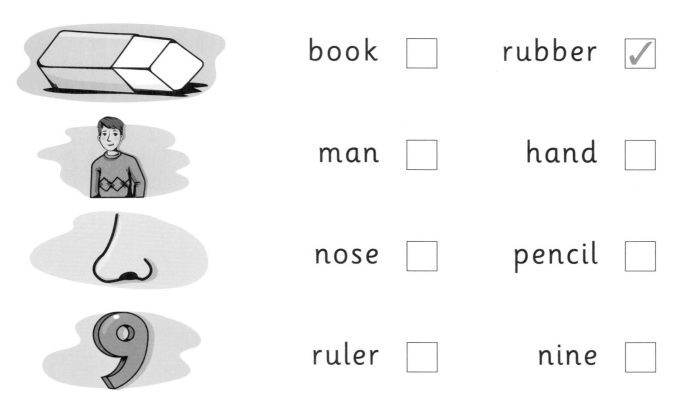

book ☐   rubber ✓

man ☐   hand ☐

nose ☐   pencil ☐

ruler ☐   nine ☐

How many n s can you find?   17

Circle the words beginning with b .

Order the letters and write the words.

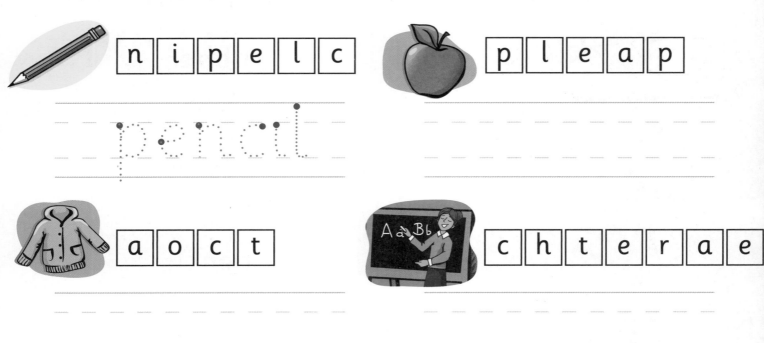

n	i	p	e	l	c

pencil

p	l	e	a	p

a	o	c	t

c	h	t	e	r	a	e

Can you spell 'fireman'

q

says q in queen.

Trace

q q q q q q q

Copy

q

Copy

queen queen u

g

says g in goat.

Trace

g g g g g g g

Copy

g

Copy

goat goat

The queen has got a goat.

Put a ★ next to your best q and g .

19

y says y in yo-yo.

Trace

y y y y y y y

Copy

y

Copy

yo-yo yo-yo o-yo

j says j in jam.

Trace

j j j j j j j

Copy

j

Copy

jam jam am

He can play with the yo-yo
and eat the jam.

Circle your best y and j

u says u in umbrella.

Trace u u u u u u u

Copy u • • • • • •

Copy umbrella umbrella mbrella

d says d in dog.

Trace d d d d d d d

Copy d • • • • • •

Copy dog dog og

Here's a dog with an umbrella.

Circle the u s and d s in the sentence.

Circle and colour the correct letter.

q / g   y / j   u / d

j / y   d / u   g / q

Find and circle.

g	bag	fingers	queen	fig
y	hello	yellow	juice	monkey
u	blue	puzzle	banana	housewife
d	cupboard	door	sandwich	nose
b	rubber	doll	rabbit	bike
p	pupil	biscuit	apple	purple

Can you spell 'elephant'

Write the sounds and make the words.

p   e   n   p e n

says **in**  **van.**

Trace

Copy

V

Copy

van van an

 **says** **in** 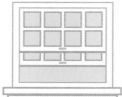 **window.**

Trace

Copy

W

Copy

window window indow

 **The van has got small windows.**

24

Put a ★ next to your best v and w

X says x in box.

Trace   x x x x x x x

Copy   x

Copy   box bo box bo

k says k in kite.

Trace   k k k k k k k

Copy   k

Copy   kite kite ite

There's a kite in the box.

says s in  sofa.

Trace S S S S S S S S

Copy S

Copy sofa sofa ofa

 says z in  zebra.

Trace Z Z Z Z Z Z Z

Copy Z

Copy zebra zebra ebra

 **The zebra is on the sofa.**

26

Circle the s s in the sentence

Circle and colour the correct letter.

(m) / n

b / p

v / w

r / n

k / z

q / g

j / y

f / t

a / o

q / p

h / r

b / d

Can you think of other words that begin with the letters that you have coloured?

Write the sounds and make the words.

u   i   c

juice

p_ _ _t

r_ _ _r

s_ _ _e

w_ _ _r

28

Write two words for each letter.

b

book

b

b

d

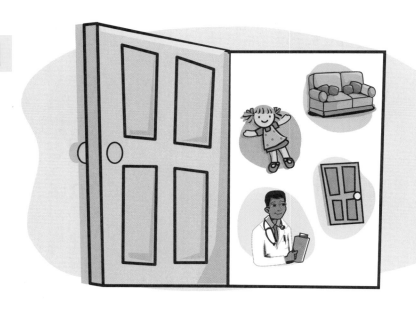

door

d

d

p

pillow

p

p

Find and circle the sounds.

sh	ch	th

teacher

shoes

bath

three

chick

fish

sheep

teeth

chair

Match and write.

br	cr	dr	fr	~~gr~~	tr

 grapes

 __ead

 __ee

 __ess

 __isbee

 __ab

Circle the ending letters for each picture.

Write the word under the picture.

(ch) ck th

beach

sh th ch

lf lk lt

ch sh th

ck lk nk

nd nk lf

A a

Trace, then copy.

B b Billy

Trace, then copy.

C c

Trace, then copy.

Copy Billy

Circle your best A, B and C.

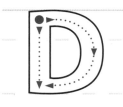

d   Dad

Trace, then copy.

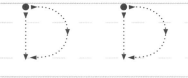

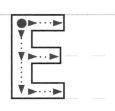

e

Trace, then copy.

F   f   Friday

Monday
Tuesday
Wednesday
Thursday
Friday
Saturday
Sunday

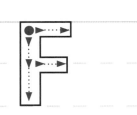

Trace, then copy.

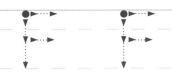

Copy **Dad**

Put a ★ next to your best D, E and F.

g   Grandma

Trace, then copy.

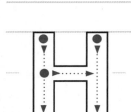

h   Hello!

Trace, then copy.

i   l

Trace, then copy.

Copy   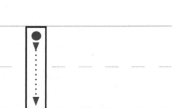 Grandma

What other family word begins with G ?

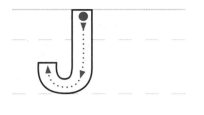 j **Miss Jones**

Trace, then copy.

K k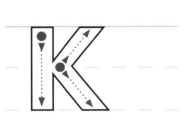

Trace, then copy.

L l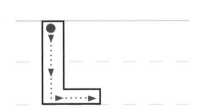

Trace, then copy.

^{Copy} **Jones**

Circle your best ☐J☐, ☐K☐ and ☐L☐.

35

M   **m**   **Mum**

Trace, then copy.

N   **n**   **No**

Trace, then copy.

O   **o**

Trace, then copy.

Copy **Mum**

Put a ★ next to your best M, N and O.

P   p

Trace, then copy.

Q   q

Trace, then copy.

R   r   Rosy

Trace, then copy.

Copy Rosy

S s

Trace, then copy.

T t   Tim

Trace, then copy.

U u

Trace, then copy.

Copy **Tim**

Put a ★ next to your best S, T and U.

V   v

Trace, then copy.

W   w Wednesday

Monday
Tuesday
Wednesday
Thursday
Friday
Saturday
Sunday

Trace, then copy.

X   x

Trace, then copy.

Copy   Wednesday

What's your favourite day of the week?

39

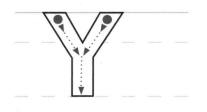

y   Yes

Trace, then copy.

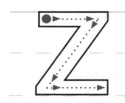

z

Trace, then copy.

Copy   Yes

Read the signs.

What are the first letters of your name?

Circle the capital letters.

Hello, everyone!

Tiny Ted is Billy's teddy.

Do you like my T-shirt?

I know my ABC.

Write the capital letters.

T	W	R	G	M

W hat's your name?

___im is ___osy's cousin.

___iss Jones is a teacher.

___oodbye, everyone!

Write two sentences and circle the capital letters.

Write the missing letters in the alphabet train.

A B __ D __ F __ H __ J __ L __

N __ P __ R __ T __ V __ X __ Z

Write the missing letters in the alphabet train.

a b c __ e __ g __ i __ k __ m

__ o __ q __ s __ u __ w __ y __

42

Write the names in alphabetical order.

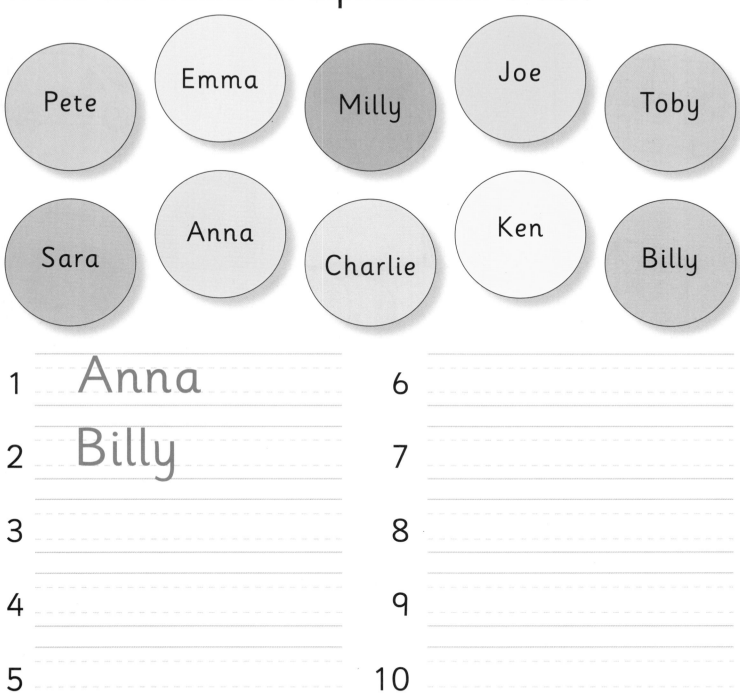

1 Anna

2 Billy

3

4

5

6

7

8

9

10

Write the name of your teacher.

Write the words in alphabetical order.

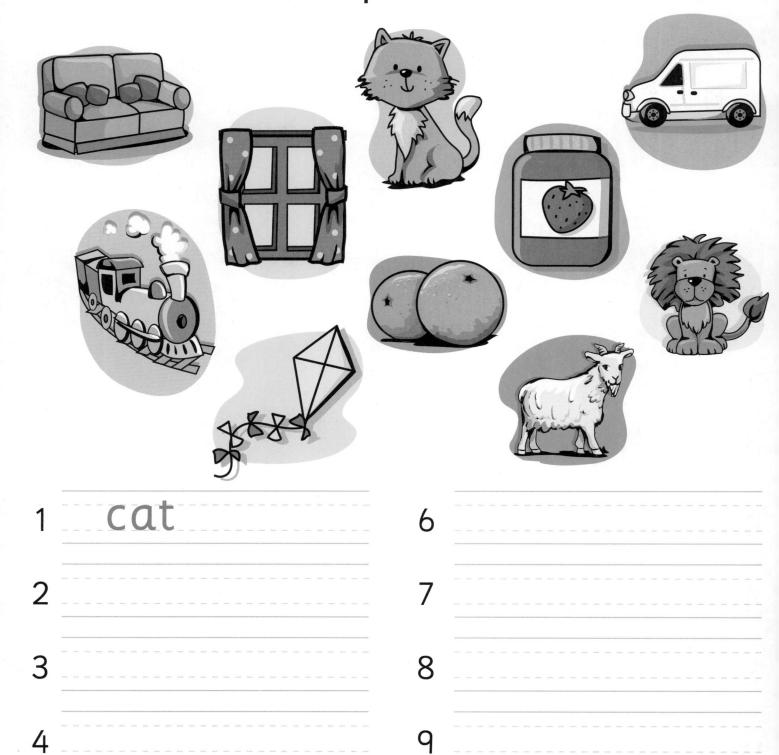

1 cat

2

3

4

5

6

7

8

9

10

Write the words to finish the rhymes.

box dish hat ~~house~~ lake tree

I am a mouse.

I live in a house.

I am a cat.

I live in a _____

I am a fox.

I live in a _____

I am a fish.

I live in a _____

I am a snake.

I live in a _____

I am a bee.

I live in a _____

Write your name

...on the book.

...on the board.

...in the card.

...on the picture.

Family and Friends
Alphabet Book

Alphabet award to

_____

_____

Well done!

OXFORD
UNIVERSITY PRESS

Great Clarendon Street, Oxford OX2 6DP

Oxford University Press is a department of the University of Oxford.
It furthers the University's objective of excellence in research, scholarship,
and education by publishing worldwide in

Oxford New York

Auckland Cape Town Dar es Salaam Hong Kong Karachi
Kuala Lumpur Madrid Melbourne Mexico City Nairobi
New Delhi Shanghai Taipei Toronto

With offices in

Argentina Austria Brazil Chile Czech Republic France Greece
Guatemala Hungary Italy Japan Poland Portugal Singapore
South Korea Switzerland Thailand Turkey Ukraine Vietnam

OXFORD and OXFORD ENGLISH are registered trade marks of
Oxford University Press in the UK and in certain other countries

ISBN: 978 0 19 480250 5

Printed in China

ACKNOWLEDGEMENTS

Illustrations by: Simon Clare Creative Workshop Limited pp 6, 7, 10, 11, 14,
15, 16, 19, 20, 21, 24, 25, 26, Amanda Enright/Advocate Limited pp 2, 8, 9, 12,
17, 18, 22, 23, 27, 28, 29, 30, 31, 33, (days of the week), 39, 40, 42, 44, 45, 46
Tomek Giovanis and Christos Skaltsas pp 4, 33 (Rosy's Dad), 34, 35, 36, 41.